PET PERSPECTIVES

First Facts®

A REPTILE'S VIEW OF THE WORLD

BY FLORA BRETT

CAPSTONE PRESS
a capstone imprint

First Facts are published by Capstone Press,
1710 Roe Crest Drive, North Mankato, Minnesota 56003
www.capstonepub.com

LIBRARY OF CONGRESS CATALOGING-IN-PUBLICATION DATA

Brett, Flora, author.
A reptile's view of the world / by Flora Brett.
pages cm.—(First facts. Pet perspectives)
Summary: "From a reptile's point of view, tells about reptile senses, providing insight
into reptile behavior and abilities"—Provided by publisher.
Audience: Ages 5-7
Audience: K to grade 3
Includes bibliographical references and index.
ISBN 978-1-4914-5051-2 (library binding)
ISBN 978-1-4914-5089-5 (eBook PDF)
1. Reptiles—Juvenile literature. I. Title.
QL644.2.B77 2016
597.9—dc23   2014044748

EDITORIAL CREDITS

Carrie Braulick Sheely, editor; Tracy Davies McCabe, designer;
Katy LaVigne, production specialist

PHOTO CREDITS

Capstone Studio: Karon Dubke, 17; Dreamstime: Marzanna Syncerz, 18 (bottom), Ryan
Pike, 7, Stanko Mravljak, 11; Science Source: Kenneth M. Highfill, 8; Shutterstock:
Andrew Bignell, 13, Camilo Torres, 4, Cathy Keifer, 15, D. Kucharski K. Kucharska, 19
(bottom), Dmitrijs Mihejevs, 9, Dobermaraner, 20, Eric Isselee, 6, fivespots, 18 (top),
19 (top), Lipowski Milan, cover, 1, NatalieJean, 5 (inset), Paul Reeves Photography, 5,
Vitaly Titov & Maria Sidelnikova, 21
Design Element: Shutterstock: **007**

Printed in China by Nordica
0415/CA21500544
042015   008845NORDF15

TABLE OF CONTENTS

REPTILES BIG AND SMALL

What do turtles, snakes, and alligators have in common? We are all reptiles. Even though we look different, we all breathe air, have backbones, and are cold-blooded.

We have been walking and swimming on Earth for a very long time. The earliest reptiles lived 340 million years ago!

Reptiles are distant relatives of dinosaurs.

reptile—a cold-blooded animal that breathes air and has a backbone; most reptiles have scales

cold-blooded—having a body temperature that changes with the surroundings

5

TEETH, TAILS, AND SCALES

We hold and kill prey with our teeth, so it's a good thing our teeth grow back if they break! Some of us even have tails that grow back! Tails help us balance and defend against predators.

We have tough scales that protect our bodies. Our scales vary in size and shape. Our super-sensitive skin senses touch, pain, heat, and cold.

Scales are made up of keratin. This hard material also makes up people's fingernails!

prey—an animal hunted by another animal for food

predator—an animal that hunts other animals for food

scale—one of many small, hard pieces of skin that cover an animal's body

SUPER SIGHT

Most of us have good eyesight. Our field of vision depends on where our eyes are on our heads. A snapping turtle's eyes face forward. Many lizards have eyes on each side of their heads. A chameleon's eyes move separately to see in two directions at once.

The green iguana has a third eye on top of its head. It doesn't look like an eye, but it senses movement and changes in light.

field of vision—the entire area that can be seen without moving the eyes; animals with a wide field of vision can see to the front and sides at one time

lizard—a type of reptile with four legs, a long body, and a long, tapered tail

9

TERRIFIC TONGUES

Our tongues do a lot more than taste! We use them with the Jacobson's organ on the roof of our mouths to smell and find food. The Jacobson's organ senses and identifies smells from food and other reptiles. We move our tongues in and out when we're curious about something nearby.

Jacobson's organ— an organ on the roof of the mouth of a reptile; the tongue picks up scents and carries them to the Jacobson's organ

SAY WHAT?

Reptiles' hearing is not as strong as people's. Lizards have ears on the outside of their heads. Their ears pick up sounds from the air. Snakes don't have ears you can see. They "hear" by feeling vibrations in the ground. A snake's skin, muscles, and bones carry the vibrations to the inner ear.

Reptiles don't say much either. Geckos are one of the few reptiles that use sound to communicate. They chirp and make clicking sounds when they're upset.

Some studies suggest that snakes can sense sound waves traveling in the air.

ear of bearded dragon

vibration—a fast movement back and forth

communicate—to pass along thoughts, feelings, or information

FEED ME!

The food we eat varies by species. Bearded dragons, leopard geckos, and many other lizards eat bugs. Corn snakes eat mice.

We have very slow digestive systems. Compared to other animals, we may eat less often. But how much and how often a reptile should eat depends on its species. Be sure you know how to feed your new pet reptile before taking it home!

Pet turtles that live mostly in water usually eat both plants and meat. But pet tortoises usually have plant-based diets. These turtles live mainly on land.

species—a group of animals with similar features

FEELING AT HOME

Different reptiles need different habitats. Terrariums and aquariums work for most geckos and turtles. Cages that allow airflow are better for chameleons. All reptiles need fresh water and light in their homes. Some pets may also need extra heat from a heat mat or light bulb.

Rocks, leaves, and other materials make great spots for sleeping, climbing, and hiding.

habitat—the place and natural conditions where an animal or plant lives

terrarium—a glass or plastic container for raising land animals

aquarium—a glass tank where water animals and other pets are kept

17

SPECIES FAST FACTS

BALL PYTHON

diet: rats, mice
physical characteristics: boxy nose; flat head with black stripes that look like a mask over the eyes; uneven brown spots outlined in off-white and black
size: 3 to 4 feet (0.9 to 1.2 meters) long
level of care: easy
Did You Know? Ball pythons are constrictor snakes. They wrap their bodies around prey and squeeze them to death.

BEARDED DRAGON

diet: insects, vegetables, fruits
physical characteristics: can have one of many body colors, such as green, tan, yellow, or red; triangle-shaped head with spikes; spiky scales under the chin that look like a beard when puffed up
size: 2 feet (0.6 m) long
level of care: medium
Did You Know? Sometimes bearded dragons look like they're waving. When they lift a front leg up and wave it, they are being shy.

BLUE-TONGUED SKINK

diet: dark, leafy greens, variety of vegetables and meats
physical characteristics: broad, flat body; short legs and tail; smooth, overlapping scales; dark bands on top; large, blue tongue
size: 1.5 to 2 feet (0.5 to 0.6 m) long
level of care: medium
Did You Know? Unlike many reptiles, blue-tongued skinks seem to like being handled.

CORN SNAKE

diet: mice, rats, birds, bird eggs
physical characteristics: one of many colors, including brown, orange, red, yellow, and tan with large, dark blotchy patterns on back
size: 4 to 5.5 feet (1.2 to 1.7 m) long
level of care: easy
Did You Know? Corn snakes have been bred for many years. They now come in hundreds of colors and patterns. One kind even looks like it has no scales on top!

LEOPARD GECKO

diet: mealworms, crickets

physical characteristics: flat bodies; thick tails; large heads with big, round eyes; bodies can have one of many patterns and colors

size: 7 to 10 inches (18 to 25 centimeters) long

level of care: easy

Did You Know? A leopard gecko's thick tail can break off if a predator grabs it. The tail twitches even after it falls off to trick the predator into chasing it! The tail usually grows back in a few months.

RED-EARED SLIDER

diet: floating food pellets available from pet stores; small live fish; leafy greens and vegetables

physical characteristics: shell looks like an upside-down bowl with small plates outlined in yellow; green head, neck, and legs with yellow stripes; yellow bottom shell with dark, round spots; red ear mark on each side of the head

size: 1 foot (0.3 m) long

level of care: hard

Did You Know? Red-eared sliders get their name from the red patches on both sides of their heads.

GLOSSARY

aquarium (uh-KWAYR-ee-uhm)—a glass tank where water animals and other pets are kept

cold-blooded (KOHLD-BLUH-duhd)—having a body temperature that changes with the surroundings

communicate (kuh-MYOO-nuh-kate)—to pass along thoughts, feelings, or information

field of vision (FEELD OF VIZH-uhn)—the entire area that can be seen without moving the eyes; animals with a wide field of vision can see to the front and sides at one time

habitat (HAB-uh-tat)—the place and natural conditions where an animal or plant lives

Jacobson's organ (JAY-kuhb-suhnz OR-guhn)—an organ on the roof of the mouth of a reptile; the tongue picks up scents and carries them to the Jacobson's organ

lizard (li-ZURD)—a type of reptile with four legs, a long body, and a long, tapered tail

predator (PRED-uh-tur)—an animal that hunts other animals for food

prey (PRAY)—an animal hunted by another animal for food

reptile (REP-tile)—a cold-blooded animal that breathes air and has a backbone; reptiles have scales

scale (SKALE)—one of many small, hard pieces of skin that cover an animal's body

species (SPEE-sheez)—a group of animals with similar features

terrarium (tuh-RER-ee-uhm)—a glass or plastic container for raising land animals

vibration (vye-BRAY-shuhn)—a fast movement back and forth

READ MORE

Peterson, Megan Cooley. *Show Me Reptiles.* My First Picture Encyclopedias. North Mankato, Minn.: Capstone Press, 2013.

Thomas, Isabel. *Remarkable Reptiles.* Extreme Animals. Chicago: Raintree, 2013.

Weber, Belinda. *Reptiles.* Discover Science. Boston: Kingfisher, 2014.

INTERNET SITES

FactHound offers a safe, fun way to find Internet sites related to this book. All of the sites on FactHound have been researched by our staff.

Here's all you do:

Visit *www.facthound.com*

Type in this code: 9781491450512

Super-cool stuff!

Check out projects, games and lots more at
www.capstonekids.com

Critical Thinking Using the Common Core

1. There are many types of reptiles. What are three features all reptiles have in common? (Key Ideas and Details)

2. Reptiles are super sniffers! How do reptiles use their sense of smell to stay alive and safe? (Key Ideas and Details)

3. Why do you think it's so important to provide reptile pets with the right food and habitat? (Integration of Knowledge and Ideas)

INDEX